T0121021

Durvue
New Language
- Dictionary

Durga Madiraju

authorHOUSE®

AuthorHouse™
1663 Liberty Drive
Bloomington, IN 47403
www.authorhouse.com
Phone: 833-262-8899

Published by AuthorHouse 01/09/2023

ISBN: 978-1-6655-7948-3 (sc)
ISBN: 978-1-6655-7947-6 (e)

Print information available on the last page.

This book is printed on acid-free paper.

Author Info

Education Qualifications:
BS Accounting - Osmania University
MA Economics – University of Hyderabad
MBA (Accounting Information Systems) – Eastern Michigan University
MS Information Systems – Eastern Michigan University
PhD in Business Administration - Last Phase of Research

Certifications:
Certified in Executive Leadership and High-Performance Leadership –
Cornell University
Certified in Executive Business Analytics - MIT
Certified Scrum Master (Scrum Alliance) - 2015
Certified in Six-Sigma Green Belt and Green-Belt Growth - 2011
Lean Certified – 2013
Certified in Applied Machine Learning - Columbia Engineering
School - 2022

Author:12 Poetry Classics:
Seasonal Woods,
Summer Woods,
Autumn Woods,
Winter Woods,
Springtime Woods.
Mid-Summer Woods,
Woods, a Summer Weave
Woods an Autumn Weave Gold
Woods A Spring Weave Silver

Woods An Art
Woods A Solitude
Woods A Musical Path

Short Story Publication:
An Artsy Life, A Story Classic

Economic and Management Publication: *Scrum Art Handbook*

Abstract Classics (Book)
A View To A Door, An Abstract Classic

Business Communication (Book)
Reserved Words and Comments

Music Composed under the name of Jane Summers
Seasonal Summers – 1 song album
Summers Way – 5 song album
Autumn Sacred -7 song album
Durvue language - Autumn Sacred Song
German Language - Friend fur Tage!
Prayers of Peace
Lyriconnets - 12 songs (one-liners)

3 US Copyright for Business Methodologies

Awards:
AT&T Technology Award 2012
Wall of Stars Award – IT Department 2014
Marquis Who's Who America (2016)
Marquis Lifetime Achievement Award (2020)
POWER of Excellence (Women of Excellence Award) 2018-2020
Marquis Top Engineer Award – 2020
Marquis Industry Leader Award - 2021
Marquis Top Professional Award - 2022
Marquis Top Artist Award – 2022

Contents

Acknowledgements ix

SECTION 1
Durvue Dictionary

Part 1 Alphabets in Durvue 1
Part 2 Goddess Visalakovue Visalakovue Bavovue - 110 names
        (Mother Prayers) 30
Part 3 Prayers 39
Part 4 Poems 43
Part 5 Durvue Songs 53
Patriotic Song of USA Notes (Piano Notes) 56

SECTION 2
Business Rule Improvement Model

Tagging a System Improvement Rule 67

SECTION 3
New naturmed codes

Lyricones 76

Acknowledgements

This book is dedicated to my father Dr. Chinta Chidananda Rao (Chief Medical Officer, South Central Railway), my mother Chinta Visalakshi, my husband Srinivas Madiraju, my daughter Anika Madiraju, my family and friends.

My sincere appreciation to all my friends, and well-wishers who have helped me at all times.

Sincerely,
Durga Madiraju

SECTION 1

Durvue Dictionary

Part 1

Alphabets in Durvue

A - Aau
B - Bau
C - Cau
D - Dau
E - Eau
F - Fau
G - Gau
H - Hau
I - Iau
J - Jau
K - Kau
L - Lau
M - Mau
N - Nau
O - Oau
P - Pau
Q - Qau
R - Rau
S - Sau
T - Tau
U - Uau
V - Vau
W - Wau
X - Xau
Y - Yau
Z - Zau

Numbers in Durvue

1 - Aaun

2- baun

3- caun

5- daun

6- eaun

7- faun

8- gaun

9- haun

10- Iaun

11- baaun

12- babaun

12- bacaun

13- badaun

14- baeaun

15- bafaun

16- bagaun

17- bahaun

18- baiaun

19- bajaun

20- Caaun

21- cabaun

22-cacaun

23- Cadaun

24- caeaun

25- cafaun

26- cagaun

27-cahaun

28-caiaun

29-cajaun

30- Daaun

31- Dabaun

32- Dacaun

33- Dadaun

34- Daeaun

35- Dafaun

36- Daguan
37- Dahaun
38- DaIaun
39- Dajaun
40- eaaun
41- ebaun
42- ecaun
43- edaun
44- eeaun
45- efaun
46- egaun
47- ehaun
48- ekaun
49 -elaun
50 - Faaun
51- Fabaun
52 - Facaun
53 -fadaun
54 - Faeaun
55 - fafaun
56 - fagaun
57 -fahaun
58- faiaun
59- fajaun
60 -jaaaun
61 -jabaun
62 -jacaun
63 -jadaun
64 -jaeaun
65 -jafaun
66 -jagaun
67 -jahaun
68 - jaiaun
69 -jajaun
70 - kaaaun
71 -kabaun

72 -kacaun
73 -kadaun
74 -kaeaun
75 -kafaun
76 -kagaun
77 -kahaun
78 -kaiaun
79 -kajaun
80 -laaaun
81 - labaun
82- lacaun
83-ladaun
84-laeaun
85-lafaun
86-lagaun
87- lahaun
88-laiaun
89-lajaun
80-maaun
81-mabaun
82-macaun
83-madaun
84-maeaun
85-mafaun
86-magaun
87-mahaun
88-maiaun
89-majaun
90-naaaun
91-nabaun
92-nacaun
93-nadaun
94-naeaun
95-nafaun
96-nagaun
97-nahaun

98-naiaun
99-najaun
100-ooaaun
101 - aoaaun p
201 - bobaun
301 - cocaun
401- dodaun
501 - eoaaun
1001- aouaaun
2001- bouaaun
3001-couaaun
-100001 -ainaaun
-1000001-auvauaan
-10000001- avenaauan
-100000001 - averaauan

Days
Monday - vierdauve
Tuesday - sierdauve
Wednesday - lierdauve
Thursday - nierdauve
Friday - wierdauve
Saturday - Cierdauve
Sunday - jierdauve

Festivals
Christmas - Ziemavex
New year - Nouvier
Diwali - Mavalea
Sankranti - modevei
Ugadi - gavami
Karthika Pournami - kavarovue movara

Geographical Position
North - Avonov
South - kavonov
East - davonov
West - mavanov

Colors
Quaov - Black
Cuaov- White
Tuaov- Blue
Luaov- Pink
Muaov - Purple
Fuaov - yellow
Ruaov - Red
Bruaov - Brown

Fruits
Apple - cavolo
Bananas - Bavono

Blueberry - kaveovery
Grapes - vapreo
Blackberry - Navreovery
Oranges - avereo
Lemon - lemereo
Mangoes - Mangereo
Strawberry - Stauvereo

Vegetables
Tomatoes - yosavo
Potatoes - bevazo
Onions - omiove
Peas - peauve
Carrots - caravue
Okra - bendaov
Eggplant - Cevagel
Spinach - Greemaovue

Grains
Lentils - leviel
Rice - sevie
Wheat - beveat
Beans - Ventiel

Seasons
Spring - Spraovovue
Summer - Sumovue
Winter - winvovue
Autumn - Amovue

Animals
Dog - Zaug
Cat - besaut
Bird - Bierd
Parrot - sevarvet
Cuckoo - cuckovue

Dove - zavove
Lion - Kavion
Tiger - Diver
Panther - Panthovue
Rat - Vart
Bear - Bevear

Math
Add - vavaud
Divide - devaud
Multiply - melvaud
Count - cuvaud
Subtract - subaud
Equation - Equavaline

Opposites
True - druev
False - favel
Positive - povitev
Negative -negvitev

Day
Day - Dauve
Night - Nachvaouve
Evening - cevenouve
Afternoon - vaterouve
Days - Dauven

Sun - Suverwei
Moon - Mumervei
Stars - Nakasovue
Sky - akasouve

Nakasovue
Visalakoue nakasovue
Anikaovue nakasovue
Chidanandovue nakasovue

Durgaovue Nakasovue
Srinivasovue Nakasovue

Masaovue
Januaovue
Febraovue
Marsaovue
Apraovue
Mayovue
Junovue
Julovue
Augovue
Septovue
Octovue
Novovue
Decovue

Verbs and verb tense

Is - isav
Must - wiest
Live - kevel
Can - cav
Could - Ceav
Can't - caver
Give - divew
Gave - davel
Will - Ewer
For - Fov
Fell - vesa
Forgot - Savia
Forgive - averovue
Forgave - averave
After - Amev
And - Anou
Ask - Aver
All - Allev
No - Nao
With - sewit
Beside - Caviev
Near - Lavier
Far - avar
Yes - wev
Why - yevei
When - yevel
Where - yevelo
Because - zevauve
Below - sevelow
Above - avelow
Willing - tavale
Again - savea
What - aveiv
We - wev
Have - hauve

Be - bev
Do - souv
Each - evauve
Every - Eauve
Evamervue - Endeavors

Every - evarvue
Best - Fevest
Better - feveter
Worse - voverse
Anyone - Awone
Anything - awenieve
Anyway - avenave
Anywhere - avenyevelo
Also - Saveo
It - ivet
An - Auen

Everyday - evardavue
Everyone - Evarvauve
Everything - everavtieve
Everywhere - evarvwero

Yesterday - overdavue
Tomorrow - fuverdavue

Singular and plural tense for person
Iau - I
Ieum - I am
In - imu
Him - ovuer
Her - ovues
His - ovuem
Won't - Wovat
Them - vemem
They - vavees
Their - vawier
We - wieve
He - hes
Her - mer
Be - Bev
No - Niev
You - Couve
Your - Nauer
Who - Hove
Whom - Mavouem
Whose - lavovue
Wherever - heviver
Where - hevelo
Whether - haverer
Which - saviere
While - walieve
Would - pevad
Every - vewery
By - Zei
My - miev
The - Tieve
Must - Meve

Rubies - Rabierovue
Emeralds - emeriovue

Diamonds - diamovue
Pearls - pearlovue
Gemstones - bemistomovue
Gold - golavue
Silver - Savarovue

A - Aau

An - Auen
Anikaovue - Goddess Anika Prayers
Abstract - ascauve
Abundant - amuvan
Alleviate - veliavave
Alive - aseouve
Abandon - navadeou
Able - avelov
Achievement - aveciemeve
Acknowledge - becevalove
Animal - kavilov
Annual - anuave
Adopt - sedav
Active - devaciv
Appear - jevear
Accept - ceavet
Adjust - hisavet
Anxious - bixaovue
Accept - saceviet
Adopt - adeove
Appeal - vapaule
Artistic - vertauste
Age - govue
Alarm - vegauve
Admire - revavure
Affect - bezect
Abide - avideou
Actual - vaputal
Ancient - avicient
Ambitious - bemiziouve
Abject - kevect
Afford - javore
Agree -naveov

Artificial - avitive

Aggravate - bevegriatue

Arch - varcouve

Amazed - bezaust

Abide - Levav

Accelerate - vecelarauve

Ample - vemape

Adore - vadore

Action - aczivien

Agenda - venaouve

Art - vartovue

Academy - avacedemouve

Aggressive - vegresauve

Appeal - vepaule

Applaud - belaude

Angry - vareoan

Ajar - bezav

Amuse - vemuse

Accolade - voccolaute

Affinity - vaffinitou

Aid - viave

Alike - valiovue

Aspire - beaspiviere

Affix - vegaurte

Alert - velart

Ahead - vehauve

Aimless - avieleouve

Abnormal - zemormioue

Abuse - vezuse

Apathy - bezavat

Adopt - tovat

Afraid - draverovue

Acclaim - savierovue

Appropriate - wetarovue

Adventurous - averduovue

Ashamed - asavmiouve
Argue - avargouve
Abolish - abolvovue
Apparent - vaperieve
Ajar - majav
Access - aveso
Admission - bamiovue
Admit - beviev
Accurate - ceviraute
Absurd - daverd
Absolve - bexaule
Airport - varpiove
Advance - avduace
Absence - bevience
Align - Veliave
Abstinence - bemivence
Abjure - bezive
Anaemia - anaemiaovue
Anamoly - mevolue
Andamou - Beautiful
Already - Averavieve
Alter - alveto
Apart - zevart
Apartment - zavartmeo
Apology - Veleogy
Application - cavelicavoun
Apparent - abveriouve
Appeal - vavelouve
Appear - saverer
Appetite - bevatiet
Appointment - vawient
Appreciate - vepearicere
Approach - rapourouce
Approval - raciorve
Auvicere - Sincere

Bau - B
Bud - Boue
Besauve - Blessing
Beasuven - Blessings
Bavavovue- IeunBavovue (110 prayer names)
Bed - neive
Beyond - Veoune
Benign - vesaun
Bad - devad
Baby - vaseo
Bat - datav
Ball - Balev
Bake - milev
Background -
Bank - mauvauke
Bare - varve
Blend - celve
Bland - bevald
Blame - veaume
Badge - zevaude
Book - bovave
Bull - mevez
Buffalo - vemezzo
Behave - beauve
Best - Wiest
Better - Hewacive
Bud - voud
Bid - Vied
Basket - baskaovue
Bun - pavieve
Bread - Faverd
Behave - bevauve
Bill - nevill
Bird - berde
Bell - levez
Box - Veoge

Boy - cield
Brain - dravieve
Branch - bravauce
Brand - vreand
Bunch - bevunch
Butter - sutou
Button - metov
Buy - beze
Being - vemeg
Belief - velieve
Belong - cevlauve
Benefit - cevefit
Bestow - gevierve
Beive- Be
Bevovue - Gratitude

Cau - C
Celavovue - beautiful
Geviouvue - Attractive
Ceviovue - Cheerful
Cat - facaat
Come - cov
Came - cev
Coat - covavue
Could - covo
Cheer - Ciervovue
Cage - cavege
Calculate - cavaluave
Cake - kewarce
Calendar - Cavelouve
Call - celve
Calf - valow
Calm - ceovue
Cap - ceaup
Car - cevaurve
Class - kleous
Classic - beassic

Dau - D

Davue - Day
Davuen - Days
Dress - Drevess
Dreary - breavier
Dull - vedouve
Dive - livoue
Dad - kauv
Dance - Javaunce
Dark - bavar
Date - daute
Daughter - dauver
Deaf - deave
Dear - searve
Desert - severte
Diary - levaire
Dictionary - vezicion
Dinner - devasurve
Doctor- doctorovue
Document - vocient
Dog - dowev
Doll - voll
Door - veroor

Eau - E

Eauvue - Every
Eamervue - Endeavors
Eat - ceatovue
Every - evaruve
Ever - everve
Eager - vegear
Ear - bivear
Early - averle
Earth - veartiv
Ease - vease
Easy - veasive

Economics - vecenomize
Empty - Launove
English - sevlize
Even - nevien
Eye - niev
Eyes - nieven
Eyelid - nieveovue

Fau - F
Forest - zesavue
Food - eviou
Flower - Sowerovue
Flowers - Sowerovuen
Forever - hoveaov
Friend - frierve
Father - favovuer
Face - kapouve
Fail - zavelve
Fair - sabiere
Fare - vefauve

Gau - G
Good - Good
Goem - God
Goal - Soavue
Gravieovue - Gratitude
Girl - Gier
Gain - gavierve
Gallon - balieve
Gap - havice
Garage - havoruve
Garden - maverouve
Garbage - ovagiere

Hau -H
Hathovue - Healthy

Harmoniouve - Harmony
Howavue - Flower
Howavuen - Flowers
Hevavue - Bestow
Hevpau - Respect
Havar- hardwork
Home - covaovue
Head - devov
Happiness - kavierve

Iau - I
India - Indiaovue
ill - ivelou
Impossible - bevossiouve
Important- Lovert
Immerse - cimmerze
Integer - iventer
Ink - kial
Inner - vinerv
Incense - agarsevouve
Intense - Iveince

Jau - J
Jeavue - Dream
Jeavuen - Dreams
Jowovue - Trust
Jevierce - Cheer
Jump - zevun
Jelly - gevele
Jewel - mevale
Jest - sevize
Jargon - vergaon
Jostle - xestal

Kau - K
Kite - soutovue

Kid - ledav
Kind - lavind
Key - veik
Kitchen - kevitche
Keep - meave
Keen - reave
Kilos - bielo
Kindergarten - Laudgarven
Kaleidoscope- laveidasovice
Knowledge - Vowkouve
Knit - vinte

Lau - L
Loyalty - Suvavierce
Lieva - Line
Lenivuel - Panchsheel
Leveov - leaves
Lamp - havelovue
Lit - kiel
Light - kaviest
Alive - feolovue
Levy - deviov
Lest - selver
Lesson - weveson
Lion - jaxovue
Late - saweler
Liver - gevorov
Livid - agvier

Mau - M
Mievue - My
Maovue - Must
Mumervei - Moon
Mother - Mamov
Sister - seasover
Brother - Bravover

Mellow - vellouv
Met - revet
Meet - reveet
Murmur - vurvure
Mind - viende
Men - Meven
Myself - bevier

N
Niervei - Night
Nothing - Autine
Now - nietz
Nocturnal - novertuneouve
Null -veoul
Nail - vail
Narrow - Verauve
Nation - navution
Name - naven
Negotiation - neverionan
National - nautionaouve

Oau - O
Ovue - Of
Ovuren - Others
Okra - laweove
Oath - Ovat
Object - ovece
Objective - covecive
Occurrence - vaucerence
Occupation - vokupien
Origin - vaurivin
Occasional - bocavision

Pau - P
Pavavue - Fruits
Pleauce - Please

Peauce - Peace
Prauvue - Prayer
Prauvuen - Prayers
Parpeovue - Prosperous
Pace - vavice
Pack - mevauce
Page - labiece
Pad - favoud
Pain - nevaine
Pace - wevauce
Packed - laveire
Pacify - bevaut

Qua - Q
Quail - Tielve
Quiz - vieze
Quit - wiest
Quilt - auvailve
Quirk - tewirve
Quest - gaviereve
Quality - waultive
Quick -avauce
Quay - javauve
Quip - revipive

Rau - R -
Revaovue - Remember
Rose - Rose
Radiance - bavance
Radio - berow
Reasonable - reseaomav
Reason - reseaov
Retrospective - restrioverce
Reinforcement -bevenceove
Run - vierve
Ran - vaverve
Rabbits - ravioute

Rule - Uvuer
Rules - Uvueren

Sau - S
Suverwei - Sunrise
Somavue - Summer
Sucavue - Success
Suwisei - Sunset
Sunav - Song
Swim - wavovue
Swan - dawen
Sacred - sucauve
Safe - vesauve
Salt - biele
Sad - vierve
Sand - tasanauve
Soil - bevovue

Tau - T
Tieva- Thee
Tievum - Today
tieuvue - few
Tie - pavue
Things - Tienve
Time - Tieve
The - Tiev
Table - veboule
Tail - tevaile
Take - devauk
Talent - taveleve
Talk - talouve
Tactful - tecauve

Uau - U
Uvuer - Rule
Uvueren - Rules

Umbrella - wevenovue
Use - viuevue
User - ievuer
Uncle - vonvel
Unable - uvale
Under - bierve
Ubiquitous - taviquivice
Unique - tavinovue

Vau - V
Visalaksovue - Prayers (For Married Ladies)
Vase - tabouve
Valance - meveaovue
Vet - bave
Van - Zevou
Voyage - bevoyauve
Visit - mivest
Vocal - bovauce
View - berieve
Vacation - bavacieve
Vaccine - mavacieve
Voile - cevoive
Violet - violeve

Wau - W
Woods - davoov
Waist - vaive
Wage - heawe
Wait - weiv
Waiter - searver
Waive - weiverve
Wave - Wieve
Walk - telav
Wander - wovear
Wallet - jelev
Want - tavet

War - dawer
Warm - favarm
Warmth - favarmev
Warn - cevarv
Wash - vaserv
Waste - newast
Watch - xavaw
Water - bevers
Wave - zabow
Wax - zav
Weak - becav
Wealth - revave
Weapon - devove
Wear - ciere
Weather -seweast
Weave - zeove
Web - Levorovue
Wedding - tevedovue
Weed - zeew
Week - keave
Weekend - Taweeve
Weekly - Paverve
Weigh - sedvea
Weight - owerve
Welcome - teovome
Welfare - beweleve
Well - leveowe
Well-being -wevibevouve
Whatever - wowierve
Wheel - pavelve
Whisper - sierver
Whistle - hiestle
Whole - quaovel
Wide - tevith
Width - tadiev
Wife - ziev

Wild - liaow
Wildlife - faviereve
Win - mies
Wind - ranoea
Windchill - lievave
Window - belaow
Wing - savaw
Wipe - raverv
Wire - pevar
Wisdom - zomov
Wide - laviea
Wish - sovase
Women - speasov
Women - speasoven
Wood - awaovue
Wool - kawoa
Work - hierv
Write - wrierve
Writer - wreaver
Wrong - lavoue
Worry - xaray
Worse - javero
Worship - uverisov
Worth - Moverovue
Wound - kalaovue
Wrap - govierovue
Wrath - bacer
Wreck - lenove
Wrinkle - Pavien
Wrist - tavierovue
Work - be wore

Xau - X
Xauvue - shoe
Xauvuen - Shoes
X-ray - Vasrovue

Yau - Y

Yavovue - Bank
Yaviez - Service
Yawovue- Dusk
Yard - havaovue
Yawn - wawavue
Year - uvouve
Yell - Bavelovue
Yet - hetz
Young - xang
Your - kever
Yourself - keverese
Youth - yaverovue
Yavovue - Bank
Yaviez - Service
Yaweive - Dusk

Zau - Z

Zeverovue - Jewelry
Zeve - Yacht
Zeuem - Necklace
Zeur - Ear Rings, ear studs
Zenith - keivavue
Zero - Zeovue
Zip - jesivue
Zoo - zovue
Zenith - bevite

Part 2

Goddess Visalakovue Visalakovue Bavovue - 110 names (Mother Prayers)

1. suwervei, anikachamantovue avovue! (Goddess, a new name of a flower, chamanti, another name of Goddess Durga)
2. suwervei, upakaouvue avovue! (useful)
3. suwervei, dhanouvue avovue! (Prosperity)
4. suwervei, paropakaovue avovue! (Helpful)
5. suwervei, sahanaovue avovue! (patience)
6. suwervei, kutumbaovue avovue! (Family)
7. suwervei, prasannaovue avovue! (praise)
8. suwervei, kashtasukovue avovue! (Good and bad times)
9. suwervei, bandhovue avovue! (Relations)
10. suwervei, subakaryaovue avovue! (new beginnings)

11. suwervei, dhanyaouve avovue! (Grains)
12. suwervei, raagovue avovue! (Raga)
13. suwervei, namartaouve avovue! (Soft mild)
14. suwervei, saantavovue! (Peaceful)
15. suwervei, akaasaouve avovue! (Sky)
16. suwervei, vaanouve avovue! (Rain)
17. suwervei, pallaovue avovue! (Fruits)
18. suwervei, sarvaouve avovue! (All)
19. suwervei, upassouve avovue! (Devotee)
20. suwervei, sahanaouvue avovue! (Tolerance)
21. suwervei, panchamiovue avovue! (Good Star)
22. suwervei Samsarouve (family relation) avovue
23. suwervei, sarvasampurnouvue avovue! (All ways good)
24. suwervei, manchiovue! (Very nice)
25. suwervei, matruaouvue avovue! (Motherly)
26. suwervei, punyamouvue avovue! (Blessed)
27. suwervei, suprasnouve avovue! (Very Pleasant)
28. suwervei, gandaouve avovue! (Fragrance full)
29. suwervei, nischitaovue avovue! (Committed)
30. suwervei, nijamouve avovue! (Truthful)
31. suwervei, pratibhaovue avovue! (Peaceful)
32. suwervei, dhyryaovue avovue! (Courage)
33. suwervei, dayamouve avovue! (Considerate)
34. suwervei, danaouve avovue! (Charitable)
35. suwervei, kaantaouve avovue! (Light)
36. suwervei, bhadyatouve avovue! (Reponsible)
37. suwervei, buddhibalamovue avovue! (Wisdom)
38. suwervei, gyaanaovue avovue! (Knowledge)
39. suwervei, aakaouvue avovue!
40. suwervei, purnimaovue avovue! (Full
41. Moon)
42. suwervei, suryaovue avovue! (Sunrise)
43. suwervei, maanaouvue avovue! (human)
44. suwervei, puvvaovue avovue! (Flower)
45. suwervei, mallikaovue avovue! (fruit)
46. suwervei, pataouvue avovue! (Song)

47. suwervei, ammaovue avovue! (Mother)
48. suwervei, putrikaovue avovue! (Daughter)
49. suwervei, ragaovue avovue! (musical notes)
50. suwervei, Puvupaliouve avovue! (As pure as a flower and milk)
51. suwervei, panchamruvouve avovue! (As swee as Honey)
52. suwervei, satyaouve avovue! (Truthful)
53. suwervei, kamalouve avovue! (Grace of a lotus)
54. suwervei, amrudraksavaouve avovue! (A honey nectar of grapes)
55. suwervei, prakritaovue avovue! (Nature)
56. suwervei, vidyabaovue avovue! (Education)
57. suwervei, nirmalovue avovue! (Serene)
58. suwervei, nishkalaovue avovue! (Flawless)
59. suwervei, kutumbaouve avovue! (Family type)
60. suwervei, sahayamovue avovue! (Helpful)
61. suwervei, nidanaovue avovue! (peaceful)
62. suwervei, kumkumovue avovue! (A bindi signifies a married lady)
63. suwervei, pasupovue avovue! (Wear a sacred yellow thread)
64. suwervei, sraddaovue avovue! (Focus)
65. suwervei, dharmaovue avovue! (Right Path)
66. suwervei, dhyvabkatovue avovue! (Devotion to God)
67. suwervei, sakramovue avovue! (Correctly done)
68. suwervei, sadgunovue avovue! (Only good values)
69. suwervei, uttamovue avovue! (Only good thoughts)
70. suwervei, sevaovue avovue! (Caring)
71. suwervei, vinayaovue avovue! (Humble)
72. suwervei, nidambarovue avovue! (Modest)
73. suwervei, mechukovue avovue! (Appreciative)
74. suwervei, ishtaovue avovue! (Likeable)
75. suwervei, sampradapvue avovue! (Prosperous)
76. suwervei, manavasutraovue avovue! (Good Principles)
77. suwervei, Manokamovue avovue! (Good Wishes)
78. suwervei, Siddhiovue avovue! (Success)
79. suwervei, abilsaovue avovue! (Hope)!

80. suwervei, nyayaovue avovue! (Just)
81. suwervei, Samanatovue avovue! (Equal)
82. suwervei, manovovue avovue! (Humanity)
83. suwervei, Durgaovue avovue! (Goddess Durga)
84. suwervei, Sampurnovue avovue! (Content)
85. suwervei, nitulovue avovue! (Adherence to code of conduct and rules)
86. suwervei, visalalakshimalliovue avovue! (A new name of Chamanti flower)
87. suwervei, Sukaovue avovue! (Comfort)
88. suwervei, Anukaovue avovue! (Submissive)
89. suwervei, namaskaovue avovue! (hands together)
90. suwervei, akasamouvue avovue! (Respect of Sky)
91. suwervei, bhumaovue avovue! (Respect of Earth
92. suwervei, abhayaovue avovue! (Not afraid)
93. suwervei, ikyatovue avovue! (Unity in all)
94. suwervei, Soukyamovue avovue! (Comfort of words or any)
95. suwervei, bhavaovue avovue! (Expressions)
96. suwervei, parampaovue avovue! (Customs)
97. suwervei, ritiaovue avovue! (Traditions)
98. suwervei, manasantovue avovue! (Peace of mind)
99. suwervei, Manchimansovue avovue! (Good Mind)
100. suwervei, ekagraovue avovue! (Anything for everyone's benefit)
101. suwervei, maataovue avovue! (Mother)
102. suwervei, pitaaovue avovue! (Father)
103. suwervei, Guruvaovue avovue! (Teacher)
104. suwervei, shisyaovue avovue! (Student)
105. suwervei, gauravaovue avovue! (Respect)
106. suwervei, samsaraovue avovue! (Children)
107. suwervei, banduaouve avovue! (Relations)
108. suwervei, sodarovue avovue! (Sisterly)
109. suwervei, nisabdaovue avovue! (Silence)
110. suwervei, harmoniovue avovue! (harmonious)
111. Suverwei Samptrutaovue (Content in life) avovue

Anikaouve dwashaouve **110 (Ladies Prayers)**
A girl must pray for all these qualities of life

1.   suwervei, andamovue avovue! (Beautiful)
2.   suwervei, naliovue avovue! (Graceful)
3.   suwervei, dayaovue avovue! (Kind)
4.   suwervei, namovue avovue! (all names)
5.   suwervei, nammiovue avovue! (Trustworthy)
6.   suwervei, nichpataovue avovue! (Sincere)
7.   suwervei, viswaovue avovue! (Loyal)
8.   suwervei, runaouve avovue! (Grafetful)
9.   suwervei, sampurnaovue avovue! (Content)
10.   suwervei, dhanaovue avovue! (Rich)
11.   suwervei, samsarovue avovue! (Family life)
12.   suwervei, vidyaovue avovue! (Education)
13.   suwervei, saantaovue avovue! (Peaceful)
14.   suwervei, garvaovue avovue! (Proud)
15.   suwervei, dhyryaovue avovue! (Courage)
16.   suwervei, vijawaovue avovue! (Succeed)
17.   suwervei, sarvaovue avovue! (All virtues)
18.   suwervei, sampurnovue avovue (Completed all)
19.   suwervei, bhaktaovue avovue! (Devoted)
20.   suwervei, punyaovue avovue!(Blessed)

21. suwervei, vijayaovue avovue! (Successful)
22. suwervei, nityasadhaovue avovue! (Always hardworking)
23. suwervei, ratnamanovue avovue! (A jewel)
24. suwervei, karyasidhovue avovue! (Successful in all endeavors)
25. suwervei, kirtaovue avovue! (Good Reputation)
26. suwervei, gyanaovue avovue! (Knowledge)
27. suwervei, santosaovue avovue! (Happiness)
28. suwervei, uttamovue avovue! (Worthy)
29. suwervei, satyaovue avovue! (Truthful)
30. suwervei, viswasaovue avovue! (Loyal)
31. suwervei, vigyanaovue avovue! (Wisdom)
32. suwervei, sarvaswovue avovue! (All Qualities)
33. suwervei, dhyanomovue avovue! (Meditation)
34. suwervei, gunavanouvue avovue! (Only Good qualities)
35. suwervei, susilaovue avovue! (well natured)
36. suwervei, namratovue avovue! (Obedient)
37. suwervei, nibbatovue avovue! (Committed)
38. suwervei, viluveiovue avovue! (Valuable)
39. suwervei, naipunaovue avovue! (Skilled)
40. suwervei, pravinovue avovue! (Proficient)
41. suwervei, gyanaovue avovue! (Knowledge)
42. suwervei, televeiovue avovue! (Intelligent)
43. suwervei, mruduvaovue avovue! (Soft)
44. suwervei, neraveraovue avovue! (Fulfill)
45. suwervei, karyasiddaovue avovue! (Success in endeavors)
46. suwervei, kutumbaovue avovue! (Family bonding)
47. suwervei, nirmalovue avovue! (Serene)
48. suwervei, sadgunaovue avovue! (All qualities)
49. suwervei, bhaktaovue avovue! (Devoted)
50. suwervei, matruaovue avovue! (Motherly)
51. suwervei, ashtaiswarovue avovue! (All ways prosperous)
52. suwervei, suprasnovue avovue! (Very Pleasant)
53. suwervei, nityasantoshovue avovue! (Always Happy)
54. suwervei, sraddovue avovue! (Focus)
55. suwervei, naipunyovue avovue! (Skilled)
56. suwervei, sambandovue avovue! (Relation)

57. suwervei, nirvahanouve avovue!
58. suwervei, sarasvatovue avovue! (Education)
59. suwervei, asweeradovue avovue! (Blessings)
60. suwervei, akhilovue avovue! (Courageous)
61. suwervei, sarvagunovue avovue! (All qualities, an embodiment)
62. suwervei, nrityavovue avovue! (Dance)
63. suwervei, ullasouve avovue! (Cheerful)
64. suwervei, namaskaovue avovue! (Prayer)
65. suwervei, bhavaovue avovue! (Expressions)
66. suwervei, anukovue avovue! (Gentle and soft spoken)
67. suwervei, Pallavoue avovue! (Fruits)
68. suwervei, Pulaovue avovue! (Flowers)
69. suwervei, santaovue avovue! (Peaceful)
70. suwervei, teneouve avovue! (Honey)
71. suwervei, anikaovue avovue! (Beautiful)
72. suwervei, balamovue avovue! (Strong)
73. suwervei, buddhibalamovue avovue! (Behavior)
74. suwervei, sundarovue avovue! (Beautiful)
75. suwervei, vajraovue avovue! (Diamonds)
76. suwervei, Kempaovue avovue! (Gems)
77. suwervei, mutyaovue avovue! (Pearls)
78. suwervei, mangalamovue avovue! (Prayer)
79. suwervei, garvaovue avovue! (Pride)
80. suwervei, gaanovue avovue! (Singing)
81. suwervei, nrutyaovue avovue! (Dancing)
82. suwervei, pasupovue avovue! (Turmeric)
83. suwervei, kumkamovue avovue! (Kumkuma)
84. suwervei, stanaovue avovue! (Bindi)
85. suwervei, Dharmouve avovue! (Right Path)
86. suwervei, guruvaovue avovue! (Respect of Teacher
87. suwervei, sishyaovue avovue! (Respect of Student)
88. suwervei, dharmaovue avovue! (Correct Path)
89. suwervei, kalyanovue avovue! (A Path of marriage)
90. suwervei, suryaovue avovue! (Sunrise)
91. suwervei, sanubhutiovue avovue! (Empathy)

92. suwervei, chandraovue avovue! (Moon)
93. suwervei, kaanukaovue avovue! (Gift)
94. suwervei, satyaovue avovue! (Truth)
95. suwervei, kalaovue avovue! (Art)
96. suwervei, pravinyaovue avovue! (Expertise)
97. suwervei, krushiovue avovue! (Hard Work)
98. suwervei, chanchalaovue avovue! (Lively)
99. suwervei, kusuma avovue! (Gentle)
100. suwervei, dhanadhanyovue avovue! (Prosperous)
101. suwervei, prasannaovue avovue! (Happy)
102. suwervei, neipunyaovue avovue! (Skilled)
103. suwervei, poojaovue avovue! (Prayer)
104. suwervei, amrutamovue avovue! (Delicious)
105. suwervei, kantaovue avovue! (Light)
106. suwervei, parijatovue avovue! (Flowers of Parvati)
107. suwervei, madhurovue avovue! (Good Voice)
108. suwervei, sarvalakshanaovue avovue! (All good qualities)
109. suwervei, sarvadeviaovue avovue! (Devotion to all Gods)
110. suwervei, sraddaouve avovue! (Focus)
111. suverwei prasantaovue avovue

God Chidanandakovue Bavovue - 10 names (Father Prayers)

1.   suwervei, manavatvaouve avovue! (Humanity)
2.   suwervei, Dhyryaovue avovue (Brave)
3.   suwervei, paropakaovue avovue! (Helpful)
4.   suwervei, sahanaovue avovue! (patience)
5.   suwervei, kutumbaovue avovue! (Family)
6.   suwervei, prasannaovue avovue! (praise)
7.   suwervei, kashtasukovue avovue! (Good and bad times)
8.   suwervei, bandhaovue avovue! (Relations)
9.   suwervei, subakaryaovue avovue! (Celebrations)
10.   suwervei, samsaraovue avovue! (Family Way)
11.   suwervei, sarvalakshanaovue avovue! (All good qualities)
12.   suwervei, dharmaovue avovue! (Correct Path)

Part 3

Prayers

Prayers of Sincerity

My prayers of Sincerity!
Mieuve Pravouve, ovue auvesicere!

Today and every day
Tievum anuv evow davovue

I work hard for success!
Ieu verosa heva tieve sucavue

imu alovue
Ovue lievow!

I am sincere in all my endeavors!
Ieuvum auvesicere imu allev mieve
Evamervue!

Please bless me God with success!
Pleauce besauve mieve Goem sucavue!

Prayers of Gratitude

Ieuvum gravouvem fov allev besauve
Uvowen mieve!

Fov eavum imu lieve

Pleauce besavue mieve wier socues

Arati Prayers

Auve Suverwei, pasapovue, lavello(Yellow)
Auve Suverwei, kumkaovue, reio (red)
Auve Suverwei Gandaovue hies (Brown)
Auve Suverwei Akshatovue siev (rice)

Samarpovue (bestow!) Goem!

chamantovue
malleovue
Samarpovue allev

dipaovue, nrutyaovue, gaanovue Samarpovue

Peauce mieve dauvovue

God Srinivasovue Bavovue - 12 names (Everyday Prayers)

1. suwervei, subakaryaovue avovue! (Good Result)
2. suwervei, kutumbaovue avovue (Family Oriented)
3. suwervei, sarvalakshanaovue avovue! (All good qualities)
4. suwervei, Sahayaovue avovue! (Helpful)
5. suwervei, bandhuovue avovue! (Relations)
6. suwervei, matrupitruovue avovue! (Devotion to Mother and Father)
7. suwervei, guruvaovue avovue! (Devotion to teacher)
8. suwervei, samsaraovue avovue! (Family Way)
9. suwervei, pravinyaovue avovue! (Skilled)
10. suwervei, dharmaovue avovue! (Correct Path)
11. suwervei, devudupoojaovue avovue! (Devotion to god)
12. suwervei, vidyaovue avovue! (Education Path)

Goddess Durgaovue Bavovue - 12 names (Festival Prayers)

1. suwervei, subakaryaovue avovue! (Good Result)
2. suwervei, kutumbaovue avovue (Family Oriented)
3. suwervei, sarvalakshanaovue avovue! (All good qualities)
4. suwervei, Dayaovue avovue! (Considerate)
5. suwervei, bandhuovue avovue! (Relations)
6. suwervei, matrupitruovue avovue! (Devotion to Mother and Father)
7. suwervei, guruvaovue avovue! (Devotion to teacher)
8. suwervei, samsaraovue avovue! (Family Way)
9. suwervei, pujaovue avovue! (Prayers)
10. suwervei, dharmaovue avovue! (Correct Path)
11. suwervei, devudupoojaovue avovue! (Devotion to god)
12. suwervei, vidyaovue avovue! (Education Path)
13. suwervei, Manavatvaovue avovue! (Humanity)
14. suwervei, Nypunyaovue avovue! (Skilled)

Nakasovue
Visalakoue nakasovue
Anikaovue nakasovue
Chidanandovue nakasovue
Srinivasouve nakasovue
Durgaovue nakasovue

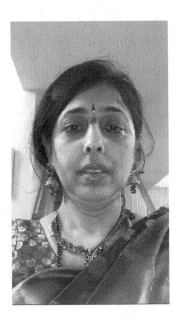

Part 4

Poems

1. **A Tribute to a Father**

Aau teraveovue tiev aau favovuer

A father
Aau favovuer
A memory
Aau memorovue

I cherish
Imu ceherovue

An advice of
Avoun cavacovue ovue

kindness in words
Sivenovue liev woraovue!

And deeds!
Anou beveeovue!

Selfless
Kavasouve

Of bestowing

Ovue jesieveon

Endless service!
Leveser sevierovue

For to see
Fov tov seouvue

The joy
Tiev jeouvue!
And happiness
Anou Kevierovue

Of others
Ovue Mouve

Is the essence of life.
Sau tiev cevisouve ovue liveiovue

2.   **The last leaf of my maple tree**

A last leaf,
My maple tree,
Forlorn,

An autumn,
A color several,
A slight green, afresh,
A slight yellow, a tear,
A slight brown, a fold,
A leaf,
I look at,
Only for
a change green!

Not any a leaf,
Empty,
All branches, My Maple!
My last leaf,
Lost,
To an autumn night!

Tis this autumn!
Only to see,
A green,
An ivy leaf, a new
But,
Not my maple!

Smiles,
My Maple,
A new!
Several, leaves, afresh,
A spring!
An age,
Only
My thought!

3. My autumn tree in my front garden

A full tree, a maple, a last, a day of summer,
Today,
A tree, a few leaves less,
A count, less, every a day!
Tis this week I saw a gap!
Gaps, branches in my maple tree!

My studies,
I Completed,
last summer!
A gap,
this autumn!
A hurry,
Lest my work,
My home,
My studies,
A disappointment!
Tis this autumn?
Yes!
A hurry,
A need!
A study,
my education,
A grade,
I await!

A work,
I fulfill,
A review,
I await!
A silence,
My respect!

My home, a glass, not broken!
My friendship, not a setback!
Only true!
I did not ignore any!
I did not fault any!

My family
Only happy!
Awaiting,
A completion, all!
For no gaps
A success,
True!

4.   A dust I need to clean a clutter

A dust every season,
I clean,
An overgrown clutter,
An Art Sculpture A difference

A piece of sculpture, An art,
A piece, several
I Assemble,
For A whole!
A painting,
Not a piece,
But
A canvas,
I paint, completely, For a view!

5.   **A quarrel, a morning and a night!**

A quarrel,
A morning,
Not a reason,
A quarrel,
An evening,
Only
For a reason,
I was ignored!

An answer,
A fault!
A reason,
Only, a habit,
I accumulated overtime!
A fault not corrected!
Only a fault
Learnt
Or taught
By another!

A reason
Of a greed,
A jealousy!
An eye
Not for an appreciation!
An eye,
Only for a
Hostility!
Only for a fault,
An appearance,
A conversation,
An education,
A work,
Only a fault I am!

A quarrel,
I cannot settle
Ever,
Unless!

Not to find a fault
Of another,
Is an answer
To a question,
A fault I found!

6.   **An autumn breeze, every an autumn!**

An autumn breeze,
Every, an autumn,
Only a breeze, of autumn leaves,
A few, for time on the ground!

Until
An autumn tree,
empty of leaves!
An autumn breeze,
An art,
My autumn path!

This autumn,
My maple tree,
Only a few leaves,
A yellow!

A green, my leaves,
An autumn breeze, early!
A green my ground,
this autumn,
An autumn surprise!

7.   **A Tree and a Meadow**

Several trees together, an acre
A meadow, several acres,
A togetherness,
A difference!
Another for a togetherness,
A Family!

A single,
An acre or more,
Only for a visitor,
A togetherness,
My comfort!

A tree alone,
Not A family,
Several trees together,
Families,
only for a harmony!

8.   An art, Sculpture, A difference

An art,
A painting, I look at,
Only
For An appreciation!
An art,
A sculpture,
I see,
An appreciation,
I study,
My hands
I use to understand the art!

A piece of sculpture,
An art,
Each piece,
I Assemble,
A whole!
A painting,
Not a piece,
But
A canvas,
I paint, completely,
For a view!

9.   A tree at night

A tree at night,
Alone,
My eyes, only to search
For a new,
A difference at night,
A new,
I need to know,
A reason,

I need
To associate
A similarity,
A difference
An experience,
A life!

10.   A dry leaf on an empty branch

A dry leaf
An empty branch
An autumn!

A brown,
Alone,
A branch,
Until,
An autumn breeze,
A path,
A difference, a breeze,
A way of life,
A season!

11.   A slope, a difference

A slope,
Grassy,
A slope,
Rocky,
A slope,
Only
Stones,
A difference,
A face!

Part 5

Durvue Songs

1.   Suverwei, Suverwei!

Suverwei, Suverwei, aau Suverwei!
C5E5G5 C5E5G5 F5 EDC

Days of sunrise, a blessing!
Davuven ovue suverwei, besauve!
C5E5G5 D5 G4A4B4 F4G4A4

Days of sunrise, a day of a cheer!
Davauen ovue suverwei,
Ovue daovovue mevarvue!
E5(3 times) F5 G5 A5(2 times)
C5 D5E5F5 A5G5F5

My day only, a focus for a task!
Meive davovue vier sevaus aau javovue!
C5D5E5 F5G5A5C5 A5G5F5

My day only for a song of summer!
Meive davovue ovue, sovan somavue!
C5D5E5 F5G5A5C5 A5G5F5

Suverwei, A blessing!
C5D5E5 F5 F5E5D5

Suverwei, ovue besauve!
C5D5E5, F5 F5E5D5

Suverwei, A Prayer!
C5D5E5 F5 F5E5D5

Suverwei, ovue Pravavue!
C5D5E5, F5 F5E5D5

A blessing every, all!
C5D5F5 black keys
F5D5C5 black keys

Aau besauve evervue aau davovue!
A blessing every a day!

Prayers, a sunrise!
Pravavue, aau Suverwei!

A prayer of trust, a name!
Aau Pravavue ovue graviervue namovue!

A prayer of gratitude, a note!
Aau Pravavue ovue gravierce, aau, javobue!

A prayer of family, a voice, one!
Aau Pravavue ovue vieci, aau nevovue, ias

A prayer of loyalty, a kindness, every!
Aau Pravavue ovue kevierce, ovue heiverce, evaum!

Suverwei, Suverwei!

2.   **Mumervei, Mumervei**

Mumervei, Mumervei!
E5(3 times) D5 (3 times)

A day of sunshine!
Aau davovue ovue suwerven
G5(2) F5 E5 D5 C5 B4

A night of moon!
Aau nivervue obve mumervei!
G5(2) F5 E5 D5 C5 B4

A night I see a full moon,
Aau niervei sieve Mumervei!

A celebration of a festival!
Aau ceabovue obve biestav!
E5(2) D5 C5 B4 A4 G4 F4 E4

A blessing every, all!
Aau besauve evarvue allevue!
C5D5F5 black keys
F5D5C5 black keys

Mumervei, Mumervei!
E5(3 times) D5 (3 times)
Aau Besavue!

Patriotic Song of USA Notes (Piano Notes)

My Country, We appreciate you!
Black key B4 Center C5D5
B5 Black key right
A5 G5 F5 E5
My Country, We thank you!
Black key B4 Center C5D5
B5 Black key right
A5 G5 F5
A voice of unity
Black key B5 A5G5F5E5 middle
In words and actions! Left Black key B4
Patriotism Is the strength
Black key B5 A5G5F5E5 middle
Left Black key B4
And the support of our nation!
Black key B5 A5G5F5E5 middle
Left Black key B4

We uphold the values of our country!
Black keys left F4G4A4,
F4G4A4B4 forward 1 time
And back B4A4G4F4
We embody sincerity, loyalty, trust and devotion in everything we do!
Black keys left F4G4, A4 4 times
F4G4A4B4 forward 1 time
And back B4A4G4F4E4F4

My Country I am Proud of you
Black key B4 Center C5D5
B5 Black key right
A5 G5 F5

My country I support you all!
Black key B4 Center C5D5
B5 Black key right
A5 G5 F5

Patriotism Is the strength
Black key B4 left
Middle C5D5E5
And the support of our nation!
Middle black key E5
D5C5B5A4 middle back
A4 Black key

My country, I belong to this nation!
Black key B4 Center C5D5
B5 Black key right
A5 G5 F5
My country Is my family!
Black key B4 Center C5D5
B5 Black key right
A5 G5 F5

Peace and Harmony is the emblem of our Nation!
B4A4G4F4 F4 black key left
G5F5E5D5C5B4A4G4F4E4

SECTION 2

Business Rule Improvement Model

Business Rule – Improvement Scenarios

Business Rules are validated either in code, in business layer or are stored as rules in the database. A lot of times, the design document or the code does not give clear examples of how the business rules apply to different areas of an application. Business Rules do not define or do not extend to impact scenarios, until a business failure occurs. Business Rules are defined within the boundaries of an application and extend to other areas but result in failures for various reasons. Business Rules must be optimized as listed in the following cases:

- Redefine impact rules to improve/simplify rules in areas where the business is having a negative impact.
- Redefine impact cases using a keyword rule with an association to other rules to help optimize application utilization and performance.
- Extend Business Rules to leverage and optimize business rule heuristics listed in the following scenarios:
  - o A map of user interface business rules to business function rules to help utilize and optimize business value.
  - o A keyword map association of one or more flows using a business improvement scenario to improve a metric verification.
- A Test Rule map to Business Rule(s) to validate and meet a test flow criteria.
- Translation of code to business rules for clear identification of business rules.
- Standardization of business rules for use by Customer Service Agents in use of application.
- Vendor Acceptance Rule map to Business Rule map, so that Vendor Business Rules are validated and verified during stakeholder review meeting.

Business Rule – Weakness

There is an impact to business when business rules are not clear, or weak, or are not understood. These rules may result in poor implementation of a system.

- Business rules are not robust, or
- Business Rules do not flow to all business impact scenarios.
- Business Rules are not case applied, if a business impact scenario requires it.
- Business Rues are not standardized where needed, such as in the case where a CSR Agent follows and applies different set of rules.
- Business rules do not negate false positives. A rule that was correct but was misinterpreted and applied wrongly, causing a negative business impact.
- Business rules do not negate false negatives. A rule that was defined wrongly and was applied causing a negative business impact.
- Business Rules fail for various system errors: For e.g.: A System unable to process due to "Retryable System Error" in the application.

Business Rule – Improvement Scenarios

- Business Improvement Rule Cross Validation Checks - Data Rule Failures can be verified through cross validation rule checks. Cross validation helps verify data rules before and after a change is made.
- Business Improvement Rule Data readiness/availability for on time is needed to avoid data failures and to complete cross-validation checks.

Requirements of Business Improvement Rules

- Business Improvement Rules need to be clear statements that can be verified using metrics showing what caused the business rules to have a positive/negative impact.
- Business Improvement Rules need to be explicit rules of metrics mapping to different flows (such as test flows, user interface flows, keyword map flows, API Flows and others.), showing a benefit for a map.
- Each flow (Test flow, API flow etc.) can have one or more than one business improvement rule associated with it.
- Business Improvement rules need to be flexible and remain an open-ended model for customization, even if the improvements are in small increments (based on Agile Optimal Scale Model).
- A Business Improvement Model must apply to different impact scenarios.
- Business Rule Improvement process is a continuous process must be used to fine-tune all areas to meet the criteria of a well-balanced application.
- Business diversification flows must also map to Business Improvement Rule flows.
- The References/Examples used in this model are based on retail system scenarios to explain Business Improvement Rules.

Business Rule – Negative Revenue Impact Scenario Examples

Some examples of business rule failures are listed below:

- Failure in transactions processing across statuses where statuses are different across systems, and business failures occur.
- Business rules not applied uniformly across regions resulting in negative impact business scenarios.
- Order Status failures that occur in different channels.

- Time latency where orders are not processed on time and do not show a status of complete.
- Use of business rules not cascading to other areas of an application resulting in business failures.
- Credit card verification checks dependent on third party tools, requiring dependency of business rules on third party vendors that create negative business impact scenarios.
- Business Rule Detail is not defined clearly in situations, where there are dependencies on third party vendors. For Example: A client is dependent on a vendor company for providing order feed details of a customer order that does not flow to the client application.
- Vendor Business Rules need to be clearly defined for any dependency so as not to cause a negative business impact.
- Data Rules are not mapped correctly resulting in negative business impact.
- Wrong Refunds made to customers
- A service was rendered but the service was not shown in the system
- Duplication of customers in systems
- Discrepancies of reports in the internal system and third-party system where the orders do not match showing revenue losses.
- Code logic skipped for certain scenarios in the application.
- Customer Subscription for a service not entered in the system.

Negative Impact of Business Rules

- Improper business rules that cause revenue loss to the company.
- Structural dependency impact in an application that causes a negative impact.
- Business Rules that are overlooked where there is a rule overlap.
- Business Rules are not implemented correctly in diverse situations.

- Defects in system due to poor business rules that has a negative impact.
- Business rules are not standardized in the system
- Business Rules are not translated into feasible metrics for verification.

Business Improvement Rule Solution Approaches

All business rule improvements are used to enhance business value for product/customer optimization. Business Improvement Rule framework must be extended to create new models through use of metrics based on economic forecasting. Some of these are listed below:

- Combine business rules with factors/impact cases using Business Rule Improvement flow.
- Provide supportive examples and use comparison studies/ metrics (test case flows) using SQL queries or mathematical formulas to show positive metrics (positive business value).

Business Rule Improvement Certification Process

- Business Improvement Rule Validity is a check made through metric analysis for better implementation of business rules.
- Each business improvement rule needs to meet the explicit criteria of a business rule defined using validity check.
- Validity rules need to have clearly defined values such as a yes/ no, true or false, or positive or negative value.
- Validity as well as Verify Rules must meet the rule criteria check defined for a use case scenario.
- Business Improvement Rule Flow can be sequential, iterative, or others based on the Business Improvement Rule Model.
- Business Improvement Rules need to meet the Business Rules/ Requirements process using Verification and Validity checks.

- Verification rules: are complete when we show proof of verificiation - Positive metrics such as order value $> \$0$ to indicate positive business value; Negative metrics to indicate negative business impact.
- Business Rules/Business Improvement Rules is a complete process when Verification Metrics=Verified and Validation Metrics=Valid; Business Negative impact=0 and Positive impact > 0; Business Goal='Met'.

Tagging a System Improvement Rule

The present disclosure provides systems and methods for

Tagging a rule in a system. The tag/keyword value is obtained based on a value or flag/indicator in a report. The tag value is defined as a negative revenue or loss or a data discrepancy or a fault in the report. The tag value identifies the data row in the database table matching the report. The tag value is renamed as a keyword and is used to define/redefine a business improvement rule in the system.

The tag value will combine the data value in a row, matched with the report (used as an identifier), and is inserted as a separate record in the system for use as an example for

- Verification purposes and
- Defining the new business improvement rules under different business situations.

A tag insertion rule inserted in the database can be used for business improvement purposes such as in the following cases:

   a.   To extend/Improve a business rule,
   b.   Create a method rule to validate an API
   c.   Create a verification file rule for form values passed.
   d.   A user story enhancement.
   e.   A product scope expansion
   f.   Generate metrics for reporting purposes

The tag value can be in the form of a new rule combining the data value in a row inserted as a separate record in a table for use in business improvement rules.

The tag value can be used as a keyword for identity purposes and can be used for improving the business function.

The tag value can be used as a check for validation/verification purposes for improving the business function.

Examples of business situations where a tag insertion rule can be defined from the report:

Scenario 1	Description	Revenue Loss
1	Customer ordered a product and customer does not exist	$200.00
2	An order was placed using someone's credit card	$250.00
3	An order violated the fraud rule	$300.00

A Value Identified in the report for Tagging purposes:

Order No	Service Date	Payment Status	Customer	Service Name	Revenue Loss
O32920208	1/2/2015	Rejected	Ann Carway	Ordered a product for home;	$250.00
046780467	1/3/2015	Rejected	Philips Snow	Credit Class unknown	$300.00

A row in the database matching the report value in the Report

OrderNo	OrderAmount	Service Date	OrderStatus	Product code
O32920208	$250.00	1/2/2015	Rejected	PRW

An example of a Failure in System identified in the database:

ID	System Check	OrderID	FailureReason	Revenue Loss
1	A check on the customers order data as well as the customer profile.	O32920208	Customer ordered the product and is not found.	$250.00
2	A check on Credit class	046780467	Order went through and the credit check was skipped.	$300.00
3	Check the Process Rules when placing an order on behalf of the customer	087654388	Order was placed by the CSR and order went through failing the product Rule check	$250.00

A System failure Verified Report

ID	SystemCheck	Orderid	FailureReason	Revenue lost per order
1	A check on the customers order data as well as the customer profile.	O32920208	Customer ordered the product and is not found	250.00

SYSTEM DIAGRAM

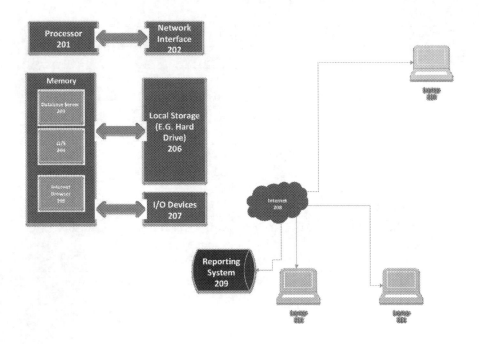

Business Flow

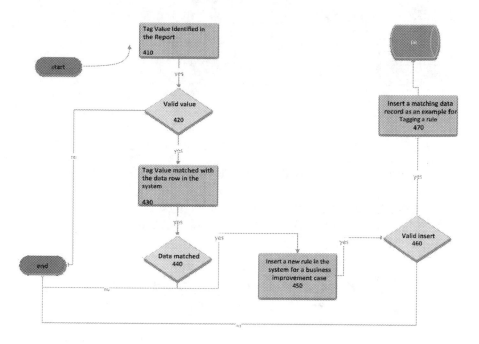

Lookup Data Record for use when identified for Tag Purposes

RuleID	CategoryID	Category Redefinition
001	520	Utilization Categories
002	620	Impact Categories
003	720	Value-Added Categories

SQL Script to insert the Tag Improvement System Rule: Improvement Table

Insert into TagImprovementSystemCheck (Improvement RuleID, TagID, FailureReason,
Rule Description(001, '520', 'Rule Validation of credit class failed',
'US20765 Simplification – Utilization Category 5201 applied'));

A Tag Improvement System Rule Example

RuleID	TagID	Failure Reason	Rule Description
001	520	Rule Validation of credit class failed	US20765 Simplification – Utilization Category 5201 Tag checked and applied

A Tag Implementation of a System Rule

SystemID	RuleIDTagID	Orderid	Order Tagged
098766	001520	087654388	Order Status successful – Rule Check Used: Product category exists and can be ordered, for an existing customer. US20765 was redefined to include the Rule and tagged and verified.

SECTION 3

New naturmed codes

Value = Comparison Metrics are differences computed as a measure of human anatomy value gains.

001 - seasonal metrics of a grain (rice) vs a processed food!

002 - Sunrise vs a sunset measure of a temperature for a health impact!

003 - Sunrise, a knowledge acquisition vs a sunset knowledge

004 - sunrise, a meditation health metric vs sunset.

005 - A difference of a consumption of a leaf tea vs a fruit juice, a morning.

006 - Comparison of eating fruits vs jelly, or juices, a health metric.

007 - Seasons, a value health impact metric for sleep.

008 - Oil vs steamed food health metric.

009 - A measure of blood flow in heart, oil vs water.

010- Leaves vs fruits a comparison value metric of different seasons.

Lyricones

A lyricon is a wrap around a song for a begin and an end. It can belong to a season, a summer for a light wrap, an autumm a cloak, a winter a heavy shawl, and a spring a light wrap.

These cones are tones of voice with no or little music, very thin to a high pitch. A seasonal summer voice that resembles a the voice of a bird such as a cuckoo, a spring, and a summer, a sound of a river and an ocean, an autumn and a winter. The tones can be mixed with a musical tone based on the level of tone and pitch.

An autumn lyricone resembles a traditional classical voice from a high to a low pitch. A winter lyricone, a tinkling dressy voice for a holiday season to welcome a spring.

Different types of lyricone wrap

1. **A single wrap**
Oh oh oh oh oh oh!

2. **A double wrap**
Oh oh! oh oh! oh oh! oh oh!
Aaaaaaaaaaaaa!

3. **A multiple wrap:**
A Repeat of 1 and 2
Oh A! Oh a! Oh a!
A sequence of a lyricone wrap with a split sec

Ahe ahe ahe
Aha aha aha
Oh oh oh oh oh
Aha aha aha

4.   **A curvy wrap**
Aha aha aha ayeeeeeeee

5.   **A linear wrap**
Saaaaaaaaaaaaaa

6.   **An angle wrap**
An angle to end a line such as a degree value is used for a lyricone wrap.

7.   **A circular wrap**
A circle I need to wrap with the same pitch for a lyricone.

8.   **A square wrap**
A square is an equal pitch on all four sides to end a lyricone. This can be for a verse.

9.   **A triangle wrap**
A triangle lyricone wrap depends on the different types of values used for a pitch, a three side equal pitch, a two side equal with the third a different value. This pitch can be used for a river sound, a lake sound and others

10.   **A heaxogonical wrap**
A hexagonical lyricone wrap can be used to mimic an ocean based on the different tides and seasons of the year.

11.   **An ocatagonical wrap**
An octagonical wrap can resemble the different architecture styles of a temple, where each can mimic an ancient, medieval or other traditional age for a lyricone wrap.

12. An equation wrap
A combination or a percentage ratio of different lyricone wraps.

13. A calculus wrap
A derived value from calculus algorithm
To arrive at a result. The result is used as a calculus lyricone wrap.

14. A step wrap
A step wrap resembles a waterfall at different levels. The pitch varies based on the waterfall speed, length or season.

15. Link Wrap
A link wrap can be used to link a pitch from one song to another for a song continuity for one emotion to another emotion.

Printed in the United States
by Baker & Taylor Publisher Services